A Catholic Parent's
TOOLBOX

Raising Healthy Families
in the 21st Century

By Joseph D. White, PhD

Our Sunday Visitor Publishing Division
Our Sunday Visitor, Inc.
Huntington, IN 46750

Nihil Obstat
Msgr. Michael Heintz, Ph.D.
Censor Librorum

Imprimatur
✠ Kevin C. Rhoades
Bishop of Fort Wayne-South Bend
June 30, 2014

The *Nihil Obstat* and *Imprimatur* are official declarations that a book is free from doctrinal or moral error. It is not implied that those who have granted the *Nihil Obstat* and *Imprimatur* agree with the contents, opinions, or statements expressed.

The Scripture citations used in this work are taken from the *Revised Standard Version of the Bible—Second Catholic Edition (Ignatius Edition)* Copyright © 2006 National Council of the Churches of Christ in the United States of America. Used by permission. All rights reserved.

Every reasonable effort has been made to determine copyright holders of excerpted materials and to secure permissions as needed. If any copyrighted materials have been inadvertently used in this work without proper credit being given in one form or another, please notify Our Sunday Visitor in writing so that future printings of this work may be corrected accordingly.

ISBN: 978-1-61278-760-2 (Inventory No. T1568)
eISBN: 978-1-61278-347-5
LCCN: 2014946470

Cover design: Lindsey Riesen
Cover art: Thinkstock, Veer, Shutterstock
Interior design: Dianne Nelson

PRINTED IN THE UNITED STATES OF AMERICA

DEDICATION

To my family and godchildren — You have taught me more about parenting than all of the books I've read and all of the courses I've taken.

And to all of the families and children I have had the privilege of working with in family counseling. Thank you for having the trust to allow me into your lives. May God bless each of you and your "domestic church."

Special thanks to Heidi Busse, who has encouraged my writing for parents and helped generate some of these topic ideas in her role as editor of *Take Out: Family Faith on the Go.*

TABLE OF CONTENTS

TABLE OF CONTENTS

TABLE OF CONTENTS

TABLE OF CONTENTS

INTRODUCTION

The Parents Who Said "Yes"

MARY AND JOSEPH are models of making difficult choices in order to fulfill their call as parents. It began even before Jesus was born. As hard as it is today to be young, unmarried, and pregnant, it certainly was difficult in first-century Jewish culture. And yet, knowing this was her call, Mary said, "May it be done to me according to your word" (Lk 1:38). Joseph, for his part, wasn't in an easy position either. It was a disgrace to find your fiancée pregnant by someone else. Yet, he didn't want to publicly disgrace Mary. So, he planned to quietly sever ties with her — that is, until the angel appeared to him to tell him that the child was from God. He then made the difficult choice to trust. He responded to the call to be foster father to the Son of God.

Mary and Joseph made sacrifices along the way. They moved to Egypt for a time to escape deadly King Herod. They endured three days of terror when Jesus, at age twelve, stayed behind on their trip to the Temple in Jerusalem, without telling Mom and

Dad. How must it have felt to pray, "God, please help us, we've lost your son"? And although tradition has it that Joseph died some time between this event and the beginning of Jesus' public ministry, Mary continued to face difficult moments, the most painful of which had to be seeing her son beaten and killed before her very eyes.

And this is why we honor Joseph, and especially Mary. Faced with a difficult task, being parents to God's son, they said "yes." And they did it with grace. But what is the call of parents today? In the Catholic Rite of Marriage, we are asked, "Will you welcome children from God?" Just as Joseph was told that Mary's baby was from God, so we are told that ours come from God, too. And what's more, St. Paul tells us that everyone united with Christ through baptism is a child of God (see Rom 8:14-17). The *Catechism of the Catholic Church* says, "Parents must regard their children as *children of God*" (2222, emphasis in original). So, like Mary and Joseph, our task today is to raise sons and daughters of God. We can do this well only through a special measure of grace. Fortunately, God's supply is limitless.

In a culture that says to indulge, it takes grace to say "no," and to endure tantrums so our children can build self-discipline.

In a time when many parents act more like peers than parents, it takes grace to set limits, and risk not being liked for a while.

In a world in which our children can be baby-sat almost completely by technology, it takes sacrifice to turn off the video games, televisions, DVD players, MP3 players, and computers and say: "Let's spend some time together. Let's talk."

In a society that sends the message that children are missing out if their schedules aren't full, it takes courage to say: "My child doesn't need special activities every night. Some nights are for family."

This is the call of parents today. With hope and much prayer, let us say "yes" as we form God's children.

"Parents have the first responsibility for the education of their children. They bear witness to this responsibility first by *creating a home* where tenderness, forgiveness, respect, fidelity, and disinterested service are the rule. The home is well-suited for *education in the virtues*. This requires an apprenticeship in self-denial, sound judgment, and self-mastery — the preconditions of all true freedom" (*Catechism of the Catholic Church*, 2223).

PART ONE

FAMILY FOUNDATIONS

Chapter 1

Seven Characteristics of Healthy Families

WHEN WE VISIT THE DOCTOR, the first portion of the appointment is usually spent checking *vital signs* — the physical symptoms such as temperature, blood pressure, and heart rate that are quick indicators of health and physical functioning. Over the past several years, researchers have identified several characteristics of healthy families that we might call *family vital signs* — indicators of good relationships and strong family functioning. If your family is doing well, paying close attention to the following variables can help keep it strong. Or, if you're struggling right now, these seven areas might be good first points of intervention to help you get back on track.

1. **The family meal.** Eat meals together, around a table, and with the television turned off. In a 2012 study, the National Center on Addiction and Substance Abuse (CASA) at Co-

lumbia University found that children and teens who regularly eat with their families — five to seven times per week — have lower levels of tension and stress at home. They are happier and have better peer relationships, get better grades in school, are more likely to confide in their parents, have healthier eating habits, have a lower risk of suicide, and have a much lower risk of substance abuse.

2. **Family prayer.** Pope John Paul II, in his *Letter to Families*, wrote, "Prayer increases the strength and spiritual unity of the family, helping the family to partake of God's own 'strength'" (4). Studies have shown that couples that pray regularly together are less likely to get divorced, or even consider it. It really is true that "the family that prays together stays together."

3. **A (reasonably) clean, well-organized home.** Okay, I'll admit this is one my family needs to work on, but the way in which we order our external environments can often reflect the order — or chaos — of our lives. When clutter gets out of control, things can feel more stressful. Take time to donate or throw out what you don't need and organize what you keep. If the task seems too daunting, break it into smaller pieces, perhaps one room at a time, and enlist the help of all family members.

4. **Family rituals.** Families that have their own traditions and patterns, not only on special occasions, but also around the rhythms of everyday family life, tend to be strong and

healthy. A family ritual may be as simple as reading children a nightly bedtime story before they go to sleep. Or, your family might have a particular night of the week that is reserved for "family game night" or other "together time."

5. **Good communication.** Keep one another informed through frequent conversations, notes (perhaps on a marker board on the refrigerator), and a family calendar. With today's busy schedules, car time is a great time to reconnect. Talk with your children using open-ended questions, such as, "Tell me about your day at school." Use fun conversation starters such as, "If you could have any three wishes right now, what would you wish for?"

6. **Clear parent-child roles.** While we want to have friendly relationships with our children, remember that sometimes we can't be a buddy and a parent at the same time. Children need firm, consistent limits that are developmentally appropriate. And Mom and Dad must also be consistent with each other. If one of you plays the "heavy" and the other comes to the rescue, your child will be confused and will have less respect for both parents.

7. **A strong marriage relationship.** One of the best gifts you can give your child is two parents who are in a close, loving relationship with one another. Take time to be together and nurture your marriage, even if it means being away from the kids sometimes.

CHAPTER 1

Every family has periods of struggle and times of smooth sailing. Paying attention to the family vital signs can help guide you out of the rough spots and make the home a place of renewal and joy.

Chapter 2

What's in a Name?

NAMES ARE INTIMATELY CONNECTED with our sense of identity. One of the first thoughts for expectant parents is what to name the baby. Our name is the first piece of information we offer when we meet someone new. Names tell us something about who we are. They can also give us a sense of mission. In our Judeo-Christian tradition, God sometimes gives a new name to those he calls to a special purpose — for example, Abram became Abraham, Sarai was renamed Sarah, and Cephas was called Peter.

Our families are the immediate communities into which we are born. The infant and young child may experience the family as his or her whole world. So, children this age have little concept of a unique family identity. However, this all changes when children first enter larger communities, such as a group of peers at school or day care. They begin to construct a family identity — the knowledge of the uniqueness of their own home and the people who are their mother, father, and siblings.

Although many influences are active in the lives of young children, including teachers, peers, and commercial media, psychological research tells us that parents are still the most important influence in a child's life during the early elementary school years. When it comes to choices about new or ambiguous life situations, even teens, whom we often think of as more in tune with peers than parents, overwhelmingly report that their parents are their primary influence for decision-making.

The family from which we come is important, and our particular families are identified by a family name. Family names are connected to reputation in many cultures throughout history. There exists a sense that when we are outside the home in the larger community we represent the family to which we belong.

Our sense of family identity helps us know we belong. It gives us direction, and serves as a compass for important decisions, especially those associated with moral values. The following are some ideas for strengthening a child's sense of family identity:

- **Develop family rituals**, especially around special occasions, but also around everyday events, such as bedtimes and mealtimes.

- **Make your family traditions and values explicit by talking about them.** For example, when citing a rule or norm of your family life, you might wish to say, "In the Ramirez family, we use our words instead of fighting when we disagree." Celebrate particular values and practices that make your family unique.

- **Connect family ideas and rules with faith and Catholic identity**. This can help your children remain grounded in the values you have taught them even during the teen and young adult years. That's when their focus shifts somewhat to the pursuit of individual identity.

- **Remind your children that they represent the family when they are away from home**. Discuss practical ways in which they show who they are and where they come from as they interact with others.

- **Create meaningful visual symbols of your family**. Hang a family portrait in your home. Find out if your family has a crest, and place it somewhere in your home as well. If none exists, work together as a family and make your own crest, incorporating symbols of what makes your family special.

The family is a gift from God, a special community created to help us learn to love God and others. Let us celebrate who we are as families and make our own family name a sign of who God calls us to be.

Our Naming Traditions

"What name do you give this child?" It is part of our Catholic tradition to give children the name of a saint at baptism. The saint's name reminds us of our heritage and gives us a practical role model for following Christ. Sometimes this saint's name is one that has been passed through the family, a sort of family "patron saint." It could be a favorite saint of the mother or father, or a saint whose feast day falls near the child's birthday. Likewise, at confirmation, it is traditional to take the name of a saint. This may or may not be the same as the baptismal name, but it is often a saint in whom the young person has a special interest due to a particular talent or quality he or she would like to emulate.

(For suggestions on saint names, see the book *Patron Saints for Every Member of Your Family, Every Profession, Every Ailment, Every Emergency, and Even Every Amusement,* by Thomas Craughwell, and these apps from Our Sunday Visitor: *Patron Saints App, Saint Names for Your Baby App* and *Confirmation Names App* [www.osv.com].)

CHAPTER 3

The Importance of a Father's Witness

As the composition of the typical American family continues to change, a number of recent studies in the social sciences[1] document what our Church has taught over the centuries. Fathers fill a unique and irreplaceable role in the lives of children. According to the research, the positive impact of involved fathers includes better grades, more active participation in extracurricular activities, better self-control, higher levels of initiative, and better parenting skills when their sons grow up to have children of their own. Of particular interest to those of us who are Catholic is the father's impact on

---

[1] For a review of the literature in this area, see Rosenberg, J., and Wilcox, W.B. (2006). *The Importance of Fathers in the Healthy Development of Children*. U.S. Department of Health and Human Services Administration for Children and Families.

a son or daughter's future faith life. Research[2] indicates that children most often follow the example of their fathers when it comes to faith practices. They will tend to choose the religion of their fathers, even if the mother and father come from different faith backgrounds. Studies also show that they will tend to participate in church activities as adults to the extent that their fathers did. Clearly, fathers form powerful role models for their children in many areas of life, especially in molding faith and character.

In 2008, Pope Benedict XVI beatified Louis and Zélie Martin, the parents of St. Thérèse, the Little Flower. A Doctor of the Church, Thérèse is known for her message that God can use all actions done in love, no matter how small, for his glory. Blessed Louis and Zélie, like their daughter, were humble, ordinary people living what the world would view as ordinary lives. Yet it is clear from Thérèse's writings that her parents took seriously one of the Church's fundamental principles: the family is the school of holiness.

The *Catechism of the Catholic Church* calls the family the "domestic church" and adds that parents are the first and foremost important educators of their children. Louis and Zélie Martin knew that if their little girls were to grow as people of God, they would need to show them the way. But when Thérèse

---

[2] Haug, W., and Warner, P. "The Demographic Characteristics of the Linguistic and Religious Groups in Switzerland." *Population Studies, No. 31, Vol. 2: The Demographic Characteristics of National Minorities in Certain European States* (2000). Strasbourg: Council of Europe Directorate General III – Social Cohesion.

was just four years old, tragedy struck. Zélie died of cancer, leaving Louis to parent the family alone. Louis had no deep theological knowledge or profound ability to bear this formidable task. There was nothing that would make one stop and say, "This man will raise a saint." What he did have was his simple faith, a faith he put into action in small ways each day as he fathered his children.

In her autobiography, Thérèse speaks of her awareness of the importance of God in the eyes of her father. She never doubted she was loved, because her father took special time with her, even when he could only afford a few moments. She also never doubted that her father loved God. Their home in Lisieux was filled with reminders of God who held first place in their lives, from the statue of a smiling Mary to religious articles among the children's toys.

Thérèse also described watching her father at Mass: "Sometimes his eyes would fill with tears he could not keep back, and when he was listening to the eternal truths, he seemed to be in another world and no longer in this" (from *Story of a Soul*). If the family saw a poor person on the street, they gave what they could. Concern for the poor became an important priority for the children. Thérèse and her father would sometimes spend time in prayer together at the church before the Blessed Sacrament, and at home at bedtime. Thérèse wrote about her father, "At long last we would make our way upstairs to say our night prayers, and once again I would find myself close to him, only having to look at him to know how saints must pray."

So what can we learn from Blessed Louis Martin and the example he gives us for fatherhood? One important lesson is that we all must take our faith seriously enough to let it touch our hearts. Christianity is not just a "life enhancement," but is a way of life that speaks to who we are as human beings. God made us for himself, and we cannot have true and lasting peace without him. To have a relationship with someone we must know them. And so it is with God. Louis Martin was no theologian, but he still had a working knowledge of the Faith. He spent time in prayer and listened to God's Word in the readings of the Mass. His children saw his devotion, and it led them to commit their own hearts to God.

Blessed Louis understood the value of family relationships, and he took the time to be with his children and to speak honestly to them. Just as he knew God, he also knew his children. So when it was time to give correction, it was given in the context of relationship, and it was taken seriously.

In his homily on the occasion of the beatification of Louis and Zélie Martin, Cardinal Saraiva Martins said, "It is in the heart of the family that parents should be for their children by their words and their example, the first announcers of the faith." God chooses to reveal himself to us as a father. So, we need faithful, nurturing, loving, and involved fathers to help us see who he is.

Little everyday things — praying together, giving to others, going to Mass, spending time with one another. These things are what Catholic family life is all about, and they provide fertile soil for the seeds of sainthood.

CHAPTER 4

A Mother's Self-Giving Love

St. Gianna Molla lived in Italy in the mid-twentieth century. A successful woman on all accounts, Gianna was a pediatrician with a thriving practice. She was also a wife and a mother of three young children. When she became pregnant with her fourth child, she developed a fibroma on her uterus and began to suffer severe complications. Doctors gave her three options: to have an abortion, to have a hysterectomy, or to have only the fibroma removed and risk her own life by continuing the pregnancy. Although the Catholic Church forbids direct abortion in all cases, it would have been permissible for Gianna to have a hysterectomy in order to save her life though this would have resulted in the death of her unborn child. She chose instead to have only the fibroma removed and to continue with the pregnancy. As a medical doctor, Gianna knew the risk she was taking. She made it clear to her loved ones that if there was a situation in which a choice had to be made between her life and the life of her unborn child, she wanted the baby to live.

Gianna gave birth by Caesarean section, but died of complications a week later. She was canonized in May 2004. Today, the child for whom she gave her life, Gianna Emanuela, is a doctor in Milan, Italy, and frequently speaks about her mother's heroic life and death.

Few mothers will be in a situation to literally give their own lives for their children, but there are many who would. Self-giving love is an integral part of the vocation of motherhood. In a society that says we "shouldn't have to" give up any part of ourselves for someone else, and that women who make sacrifices for their children are denying who they are and need to be "liberated," millions of mothers know the truth: motherhood is about *self-giving love*.

From the very beginning, when mothers share space inside their own bodies with another human being, to the feedings, the diaper changes, and time spent just gazing at their children, motherhood is self-gift. It means saying, "I'll miss some sleep to make sure you're cared for," Or, "I'll risk getting sick to hold you until you feel better." Or, "I'll put my own hobbies aside for a while to help you get to soccer, dance, and whatever else."

If you are a father, appreciate how much your wife gives of herself, and give yourself in love to her and to your children. If you are a friend of a mother, support her and offer her a little "me" time once in a while, since self-giving also means having a self to give.

If you are a mother, *thank you* for your self-giving love. Mothers know they don't lose themselves when they give themselves in love to their children. They become who they really are.

CHAPTER 5

The Power of "I Don't Know"

IF YOUR CHILD IS LIKE MOST CHILDREN, he or she is full of questions. Kids come to us because we are the answer people. After all, we are the ones who know how to pay the bills, drive a car, cook the meals, and other mysterious secrets they are only beginning to understand. So it makes sense to them that we must know pretty much everything. (This changes when kids reach adolescence, when they decide we know nothing at all.)

Many parents struggle with the first few times they are asked questions they don't know — whether they are about philosophical issues such as, "Why is there suffering in the world?" or scientific ones such as, "Why is the sky blue?" Parents sometimes feel they need to maintain that image of omniscience or their child might feel insecure, left without the comfort of believing their parents know it all.

In reality, being asked a question you don't know can be a wonderful opportunity. You can model intellectual inquiry and spend quality time with your children. The best answer a parent can give in these situations is, "I don't know, *but let's find out together.*" Then, take advantage of all the wonderful information-gathering tools at your disposal. This could include the Internet, your local science museum, a library, or a university. For more philosophical or faith-related questions, you might find answers at the local Catholic bookstore, church library, or in a conversation with the parish priest.

Embarking on this journey together helps your child learn some important lessons. One is that his or her questions are important enough to you to be taken seriously. The stereotypical chasm of communication between parents and teens begins when they are no longer satisfied with the pat (or even flippant) answers parents might give when they don't really know the answers.

Another important lesson is that when you don't know the answer, you shouldn't give up asking the question. Modeling the process of seeking knowledge helps to prepare your children to do the same thing on their own in the future. This can help them learn how to seek out reliable sources and screen the information they find. The determination you show in this process will teach them that knowledge is worth searching for.

Finally, when parents and kids look for answers together, children learn that we are never finished learning and growing. We never know everything, and if they haven't already figured out that *you* don't know everything, they soon will. Your lack of defensiveness and your honesty about what you don't know is important. It will set the stage for them to be a little less defensive as teenagers, a time when they want to believe *they* know it all. More important than how much we know is our understanding of how to ask the right questions and how to seek the truth.

The Church teaches that you are your child's first and most important teacher. Sometimes we teach not by providing answers, but by asking questions together. So, don't be afraid to wonder with your child.

QUESTIONS FOR REFLECTION ON PART ONE

What do your "family vital signs" look like right now?
What might be needing some added attention?

~

How strong is your sense of "family identity"? How
might this be strengthened though rituals, symbols, and
family rules?

~

Who is your role model as a mother or father? In what
ways are you the parent you would like to be? What do
you need to continue this journey? How can you forgive
yourself and draw upon God's grace when you fall short?

~

What are some of the "tough questions" your child is
asking right now? How can "I don't know" become an
opportunity for you to journey together and draw closer
to one another?

A Parent's Prayer

*God our Father, Perfect Parent, thank you for loving me just as
I am. Give me the grace to be the parent my child needs, and to
forgive myself when I stumble. Make our home a peaceful and
strong community of your love. Amen.*

PART TWO

STRUCTURE, SCHEDULES, LIMITS, AND BOUNDARIES

Chapter 6

"Because I Said So!"

WHEN WE WERE KIDS, one of our very least favorite things to hear from an adult was, "Because I said so." We took it to mean so many different things: "I'm bigger than you, so I can control you," "You're too young to understand." "I don't have a good reason; I'm just trying to spoil your fun." Chances are it didn't mean any of those things. But we might have told ourselves that, "When I'm a parent, I'll NEVER say that to my child." And then one day, there it was, coming right out of our mouths.

My friend Lisa, a mother of two, put it this way: "'Because I said so,' used to be the lamest answer an adult could provide. It made me think my mom was lacking in imagination and didn't respect me. Now, I realize it was a self-defense mechanism. 'Because I said so' translates to, 'it's not negotiable.' 'Why' doesn't really mean why, it means, 'what are the obstacles I need to work around or remove to get my way?' It's a power play. My response to 'why' is, 'I'll tell you why if you still want to know after you do it.' It isn't that I don't respect them or think they will understand the reasoning behind a request. It's simply that I want it done. Period. I'm trying to avoid, 'Because I said so,' because it is insulting. But really, if my children were born in the wild, they would have already been eaten by a predator because they wouldn't just listen and do what I said without questioning me."

There's a lot of wisdom in Lisa's point of view. She's right about kids who ask, "Why?" It usually means they are looking for wiggle room, not that they sincerely want to know more about the reasoning behind a parent's answer. And her response to "why" is a good one. Saying, "I'll tell you why if you still want to know after you do it" says, "I do have a good reason, and I respect you enough to share it with you." But, it also says that certain limits or requests are not negotiable, and questioning a parent's reasoning won't get a mom or dad to back down or change his or her mind.

Too much in a child's life is ambiguous and confusing. Children need limits and structure to feel safe and to have a foundation on which to build self-discipline. Their limited experience means they can't always see down the road or around the corner to fully appreciate why the limits are good for them. And that's why, sometimes, "Because I said so" is perfectly fine.

CHAPTER 7

Seasons of Discipline

CHANGE IS A MAJOR PART of all aspects of life. Children grow in their intellectual capacity and knowledge base, their ability to relate to others, their physical agility, and their understanding of ethical and moral principles. As children grow and develop, changes in parent-child interactions and limits are also natural and healthy. These changes help prepare children to live as independent adults; not only that, they are necessary if the parent-child relationship is to remain healthy throughout the transition from the early school years to the teen years.

Changes in parent-child interactions around limits naturally occur in two ways. First, there are changes in the ways in which limits are communicated to children. Likewise, there are changes in the rules themselves.

Changes in the quality of limit-setting occur as a natural response to a child's development in moral decision-making. In the early years, decisions are based either on the immediate consequences to them or on their desire to please adults. They are generally interested in doing things that will bring them instant gratification, or things that will lead others to think of them as a "good girl" or "good boy." Knowing this, we can see that we need to clearly communicate to this age group consequences to make them as immediate as possible. We can also see the need to clearly and succinctly communicate our approval or disapproval of the child's behavior. Excessive discussion about why something is or isn't allowed is often unnecessary and even frustrating.

As children get older, they become more aware of how their behavior affects others and are more able to understand and internalize moral principles. Preteens and teens often learn a great deal from reasoning about rules with their parents. But, they are inclined to rebel if they haven't had their say or if they do not understand the reasoning behind the limits that are set. This is an ideal time for problem solving together — discussing the parameters, and then cooperatively arriving at a solution. Far from making a parent appear wishy-washy or ineffective, this approach, when used correctly, can elicit cooperation from the preteen or teen even when he or she does not agree with the parent. It also maintains the parent's credibility in the face of the child's growing sense of individual identity.

As children grow and become more autonomous, it is important that we begin to separate our own preferences from the vital principles they will need as adults. We must focus our energy on what we are most concerned about passing on to our children. Rules related to safety and higher moral principles should take precedence. On the other hand, we might give children more freedom on other issues, even if we know they will make different choices than we would make for them.

When we take this approach, we send a message that we respect our children as individuals, but also that when we set a limit, it's for a good reason. We also prepare our children for adulthood by giving them opportunities to make mistakes in small matters while they still have our support. Then, they have a chance to grow in their decision-making skills so they will be better able to handle everyday decisions when we can't be there to guide them.

Knowing which limits to set and how to set them is not always easy. A good rule of thumb is "flexibility within limits." Be aware of what is most important to you, and which matters may be more negotiable.

SOME THINGS NEVER CHANGE

A few constants exist in limit-setting with children. One is the honor that children are called to show parents because of the parent's unique role. This principle is articulated in the Ten Commandments as well as throughout Scripture.

Another constant is the fact that positively based limit-setting and consequences tend to be most effective. If we tell children what we would like them to do, rather than focusing exclusively on what we don't want, they are more likely to follow our directions. If they see that following certain rules produces positive consequences, they are better motivated to do what is right than they would be if they were merely trying to avoid punishment (the latter can tend to make them sneaky, instead of virtuous). This principle is echoed in Scripture: "There is no fear in love, but perfect love casts out fear. For fear has to do with punishment, and so he who fears is not perfected in love" (1 Jn 4:18).

A third constant is that most effective limit-setting occurs within the context of a relationship. When children have a close and loving relationship with their parents, they are much more motivated to please them.

CHAPTER 8

Over-Scheduled

THE ABILITY TO MULTI-TASK — to do many different things at once — has become a badge of honor in our society. With the idea that we can "have it all" if we can "do it all," we push ourselves to take on an ever-increasing number of responsibilities, and often find our stress levels increasing as well.

It's no surprise, then, that our children feel pushed to do as much as possible as well. Kids do what they see and experience the adults around them doing, and their schedules are filling up as well. Whereas today's generation of parents might remember being involved in one or two extracurricular activities as children, today's kids are often busy every day of the week. With soccer on Monday, gymnastics on Tuesday, Scouts on Wednesday, and ballet on Thursday, there's little time to pause and wonder what these hectic schedules are doing to our kids. But if rates of childhood anxiety disorders are any indication, our children are stressed — *really* stressed.

According to the U.S. surgeon general, in 1998 about 8 percent of children in the United States had a diagnosable anxiety disorder at any given time. By 2003 (the last time child anxiety was measured on such a wide scale), that number had skyrocketed to 13 percent! Thirteen kids out of a hundred met the criteria for an anxiety disorder. That meant that their stress was so severe it caused significant harm to their emotional lives, their school work, or their relationships with others. Anxiety might show itself as irritability, anger problems, inattention (anxiety disorders are two to three times more common than ADHD), restlessness, or physical symptoms such as headaches or stomachaches. Why are our kids pushing themselves to (and past) their limits? The answer is that they learned it from us. If you feel your child might be over-scheduled (and over-stressed), here are some tips that could help take the pressure off:

- **Set some family priorities.** Kids still learn best from Mom and Dad. So, you will need to decide what comes first in your family's schedule, and stick to it. Mass and family prayer time should be high on the list. Many families also have a particular night of the week that is reserved for family time (dinner and board games, etc.). If you choose this strategy, make family night sacred, and don't let tasks from work, household chores, or other responsibilities intrude. Learn to say "no," and your kids will learn to do the same. Recent research in child psychology indicates that having regular meals with the family leads to higher self-esteem and school achievement, increased parent-child communication, and lower rates of depression, drug abuse, and suicide. No extracurricular activity can do all that.

- **Encourage your child to choose *one* (for elementary-aged children) or *two* (for older kids) extracurricular activities in which he or she is especially interested or talented.** Parents need not feel guilty for not allowing their children to pursue every interest. When we try to do everything at once, we often find we're not doing our best at anything. If it's impossible for your child to choose, perhaps the solution is alternating activities at different seasons or opting for one activity during the current academic year and one activity the following summer or next school year. Learning to invest one's energy wisely, to focus and excel at a chosen task, is a much more valuable lesson than anything we could learn by trying everything.

- If your child's school performance is declining, or if he or she shows other signs of stress, **be especially firm about simplifying the schedule.** Give your child some choices about how to do this. For example, you might say: "I'm noticing that you're trying to do too much. It's time to drop one activity so you can have some time to rest and enjoy the other things you do. What are the things you enjoy most? What will hurt the least to give up right now?" Children might feel unable to decide because of pressure to remain in an activity to avoid letting others down. They may respond, "What will the coach say?" If this is the case, offer to decide for them if they need you to, and offer to be the scapegoat when your child explains to others what is happening.

It's time for families to recapture downtime together. What good is all the "doing" and "working" if we forget what (or *who*) we're working for? When work and other commitments become burdens that take us away from loved ones, or when extra "fun" activities feel more like work than play to our kids, it's time to take action. It might mean setting some limits and enduring some whining. But, it's a fact — backed up by research and the personal experiences of many, many people — that the greatest gift parents can give their children is time together. Isn't that nice to remember?

CHAPTER 9

"Helicopter Parents" Clip Their Children's Wings

ABOUT TWO DECADES AGO, a startling (yet admittedly intuitive) conclusion began to emerge from social-science research on achievement. The most important factor in a child's later success is not socioeconomic status, self-esteem, parents' achievement, or even IQ (which had been consistently correlated with academic and occupational achievement). Instead, the best predictor of later success is *self-efficacy*. Self-efficacy, loosely defined, is the belief that one can accomplish something by working at it. If we believe we can do something and have the self-discipline to apply ourselves, we are likely to get it done.

Ironically, twenty years later, we are, as a society, getting further away from promoting self-efficacy in our children. We fail them in two ways. First, we don't allow them to develop the necessary self-discipline to achieve. Second, we make them believe they cannot accomplish things without us. Surely no parent makes these two mistakes on purpose. In fact, sometimes it is exactly those things parents do to help their children succeed that put he children at the greatest risk.

One example is the rush to develop academic skills in young children. There are a number of products on the market to get very young children reading, writing, doing mathematics, and undertaking other academic tasks. Additionally, parents sometimes seek out preschool programs that look more like elementary schools than early childhood centers, in the hope that their child will start kindergarten ahead of the pack. The problem is, the research says that these things hurt more than they help.

The two primary tasks of early childhood are socialization and the development of self-regulation. Kids achieve both through *self-directed pretend play* — something they do naturally when they have the right environment. Preschoolers who have highly structured, teacher-directed schedules, and little opportunity for self-directed play, fail to develop the parts of the brain responsible for staying on task, problem-solving, and controlling one's emotions. These are skills that are essential as schoolwork becomes more challenging and students are expected to work more independently. According to the research,[3] by fourth grade, children who attended highly academic preschools are well behind their peers in most academic subjects.

Another way in which we can inadvertently sabotage our children is by not allowing them enough autonomy to learn

---

[3] Marcon, R. A. (2002). "Moving up the Grades: Relationship between Preschool Model and Later School Success." *Early Childhood Research and Practice, Vol. 4, No. 110.* Champaign, Illinois: Clearinghouse on Early Education and Parenting University of Illinois at Urbana-Champaign.

from their mistakes and develop problem-solving skills as they get older. We sometimes hear the term "helicopter parents," referring to parents who hover around their children and anxiously direct their every move. To be clear, as Catholics, we believe that parents are the first and most important teachers of their children, and every parent should take this role seriously. However, sometimes we can teach an important lesson by what we *don't* do. By not helping, or by letting a child experience the natural consequences of his or her actions, we teach them to be more responsible and show them that we believe they are capable. This in turn helps them to develop the self-efficacy and self-discipline they will need as they grow.

Children can't always be left to their own devices. They need adults to set limits, offer guidance, impose consequences, and keep them safe. But we must allow our children to grow their wings while they still live in our nests if we expect them to soar with the eagles when they take flight on their own.

CHAPTER 10

The Safety [Inter]Net

MOST PARENTS HAVE HEARD HORROR STORIES about online dangers, from pornography to child predators, from online bullies to identity theft. In a world of rapidly changing technology, it is important for parents to take the reins on online safety. The Internet is a vast community that spans the entire world. While we may trust our own children, we cannot trust everyone who may be online. Allowing a child to browse the Internet with no supervision can be like dropping them off in the downtown area of a busy city. While they may be smart and virtuous, there may be dangers they are not prepared to face.

A second reason for protecting kids when they are online is that the part of the brain that is responsible for impulse control — the prefrontal cortex — is not fully developed until the early twenties. In a medium as fast as the Internet, this has startling implications: children may literally navigate the online world faster than they are able to think through the implications of what they are doing.

So what can parents do to stay abreast of what their kids are doing online? Here are some tips:

- **Reach an understanding on privacy.** While older children (teens especially) should have some measure of autonomy and privacy, it is also a parent's responsibility to protect them. So that they don't feel betrayed by your "checking up," let them know in advance that you will be checking and why. This may include spot checks of e-mails, a look at the day's history of visited websites, and perusing social-media accounts and text chats.

- **Pay attention.** Visit the websites your children visit, and be aware of who they correspond with via text and other social media.

- **Check your security programs.** Look for parental-control functions in your Internet security program. These functions can be set to limit access to websites and determine which types of files can be viewed and downloaded. Also, install an Internet safety filter and/or accountability program such as Covenant Eyes (www.covenanteyes.com), which allows both filtering and parental notification of sites visited. Keep in mind that these safety provisions don't substitute for good supervision, as teens are often better than adults at creatively working with technology!

- **Pull the plug on porn.** Sometimes even the most innocent searches or clicks can lead to pornographic sites. Make sure your kids are aware of this, and tell them that if something inappropriate should pop up on the screen, they should immediately get Mom or Dad to help them stop the site and navigate back into safe areas.

- **Be cautious about social networking.** Social-networking applications can be a fun way for teens to keep in touch and share information, but there are dangers as well. Some formats, such as Snapchat, are even designed to delete posted material right away, offering a degree of privacy that can be dangerous for impulsive teens. If you allow your child to use social-networking applications, set clear limits on what can be posted. Some possible rules include: no personal information that can be traced (on sites like Facebook or Twitter, for example), no inappropriate photographs or photos that can be viewed by people they don't know in real life, and nothing they wouldn't want their grandmother or pastor to read or see. Make it clear you will be perusing their social-media activity regularly, and that you won't hesitate to pull the plug if you see something that troubles you.

- **Be a parent!** Let your kids know the rules regarding the Internet, and be prepared to enforce them. Kids may object, but in the end, they appreciate parents who know how to set reasonable boundaries. Remind your kids that even if you don't see what they are doing, God does. The same standards of language, behavior, and conduct that you have set for your home apply to life online.

CHAPTER 10

BEYOND TEXTING — HELPING CHILDREN COMMUNICATE WITH PEERS

As communication is now more instant through texting and social-networking sites, there is a risk of more shallow — and impulsive — conversation between kids and teens. Here are a few tips for helping your teen avoid sending "mixed signals":

- If your teen is upset at a peer, encourage him or her to avoid texting (where messages are necessarily much shorter) and to have a conversation in person, call by phone, or write an e-mail.

- Encourage your teen to write out the message on paper first. A first draft can be used to vent feelings, and can then be revised to say it more appropriately.

- Offer yourself as a sounding board. If your teen plans to talk in person or over the phone about an important issue, say, "Would you like to go through it with me, so you can make sure you say it just the way you want to?"

- Encourage your teen to read through e-mails, text messages, or social-networking messages before sending them.

- A good general policy is to avoid saying something online that one would not feel comfortable saying in person. Sometimes the online environment can make teens feel more bold or anonymous. That can get them into trouble.

CHAPTER 11

Keeping Lines of Communication Open

AS THE LIVES OF CHILDREN AND TEENS get hectic with academic schedules, extracurricular activities, and religious education, it's important that families establish healthy lines of communication that help parents and kids stay in touch. Here are a few recommendations:

- **Remember to communicate about the positive and the everyday.** Sometimes, when things get busy, parents find that they are only really talking with their children when a big issue (usually a negative one) arises. This can lead to the child or teen associating talks with parents to being in trouble. Remember to take time to point out the good things you are seeing, and ask about things that interest your child.

- **Make good use of the time you do have together**. One often-overlooked time families have together is "car time." Create some opportunities to talk about important issues, touch base on plans, or say a prayer together while in the car.

- **Use open-ended conversation starters**, such as, "Tell me about something you are working on at school right now," or, "What is one dream you have for the future?"

- When you need to ask a question that may make your child defensive, **try asking by "wondering out loud."** For example, "I'm noticing that lately your chores aren't getting done, and I'm wondering why that's happening."

- **Take time for regular family meals**. Eating together is one activity families shouldn't give up as schedules get busier. Regular family meals have been shown by research[4] to be associated with higher grades, higher self-esteem, lower incidences of depression and suicide, lower rates of substance abuse, and many other positive outcomes.

- **Communicate with others who see your child on a regular basis**. Be sure to take advantage of opportunities to meet your child's school teachers, religion teachers,

---

[4] The National Center on Addiction and Substance Abuse at Columbia University (2012). "The Importance of Family Dinners VIII: A CASA Columbia White Paper." New York: Columbia University.

coaches, and others who interact with your child on a regular basis. This is important both for your child's safety and so that you can be aware of important things you may not hear from your child (academic struggles, social issues, etc.). Many schools and other organizations are now using e-mail and other Internet-based systems so that parents and teachers can communicate "behind the scenes" about missing homework assignments and other issues. Be sure to check on what systems exist, and get e-mail addresses of adults who work with your child.

- **Pray together**. When your family is close to God, you are also more connected with one another, even at those times when you can't be together.

QUESTIONS FOR REFLECTION ON PART TWO

When have you had to say "Because I said so" when your child didn't (or didn't want to) understand your request to do something?

~

How have your limits and boundaries for your child changed as your child has grown? What new adjustments might be in order right now?

~

What does your family schedule look like? Is your child over-scheduled? If so, what steps can you take to bring more balance to his or her activities?

~

Are you a "helicopter parent"? What are some areas in which you can give your child more independence? Which areas are the most difficult for you to let go?

~

What provisions have you made to ensure that your child is safe online? What additional steps can be taken?

~

When and where are members of your family communicating with one another? How can you keep in closer contact? Are there some neglected "together times" that can be opportunities to touch base?

A Parent's Prayer

*Dear God, it can be a challenge sometimes to set and enforce
limits in a world that doesn't always support my values.
Give me the courage to set the standards my child needs,
and help me find the balance between giving my children
direction and allowing them independence. Keep them safe
when I can't be there. Amen.*

PART THREE

FORMING KIDS IN FAITH

CHAPTER 12

Ages and Stages of Faith Development

BECAUSE GOD IS OUR CREATOR, the potential for faith is hard-wired into our very existence. But the way in which we learn about, understand, and experience our faith is different at every age and stage of life. This is why the *General Directory for Catechesis* (the Vatican's instruction on religious education) states, "Variety is required by 'the age and the intellectual development of Christians, their degree of ecclesial and spiritual maturity, and many other circumstances' " (148).

AGES 0-2

Ideally, infants and toddlers first discover God through their relationship with their parents. The relationship of an infant to his or her parent is one of complete dependence. It is through this relationship that infants learn that they are valuable, that their needs will be responded to, and that human contact is positive. This creates the potential for future relationships, including a friendship with God, who reveals himself to us as divine parent. Young children watch carefully to see what their parents are doing, and as they see their mothers or fathers in prayer and worship, they wish to imitate them, and their capacity for faith is nurtured.

AGES 3-5

For Catholic children, the parish is often one of the first experiences of society outside the home, and children's early experiences at Mass and in early childhood religious education help to form their view of the Church. Children this age learn about God in the same way they learn about everything else — through sensory experience. Music, icons, stories with pictures or props, and other activities can assist in this process. Because children in this age group are beginning to understand their identity as unique human beings, their thoughts, play, and conversation are typically self-focused. This is an ideal time for them to discover themselves as people created by God to do his work in the world.

AGES 6-12

The elementary school years are a time of tremendous growth and learning. Elementary-age children are very concrete in their thinking. So, faith concepts should be communicated to them in simple, concrete terms, and any abstract concepts illustrated with something from their own experience. This is the example of Christ, who used concrete metaphors, such as fishing, tending sheep, and planting seeds, when teaching about God's kingdom to people who experienced those things on a daily basis.

Children in the elementary grades are quite conscious of rules, making this an ideal time to teach morality from the standpoint of God's guidelines for our behavior. This will lay a foundation for conscience formation at a deeper, more abstract level as they mature. As children progress through the elementary years, peer relationships become increasingly important. While parents are still the "primary catechists" (first teachers of the faith), children this age also benefit greatly from learning about faith in a community of peers.

Ages 13-18

Adolescence is a critical time in identity formation, socialization, and the formation of adult conscience. Teens tend to be quite self-focused as they go through the physical, mental, and emotional changes of this period of life. Experiences in faith formation for teens should provide opportunities for self-discovery in light of Christian teaching and include peer-based spiritual and formational experiences. Many teens are beginning, either openly or internally, to ask themselves if they should make their parents' faith their own. They need to feel free to ask questions, and even to openly disagree. Parents and other teachers of the faith should not feel threatened by this process — it's how teens "try on" the faith for themselves. With gentle understanding and confident guidance from adults, many teens decide to make Catholicism their own. Teens are particularly attracted to opportunities to serve the poor and marginalized, and they bring fresh energy to the charitable and social-justice activities of the Church.

There is often disagreement between parents and teenagers concerning fashion, music, hairstyles, and what freedoms and responsibilities they should have. But it's interesting to note that teens report a desire for spiritual experiences and a real need for guidance when it comes to adult issues with which they have little experience. We should listen to them without defensiveness and encourage them to keep asking questions. At the same time, we should give them a strong example of faithfulness to Church teaching and an ongoing process of spiritual growth. With this approach, teens will often respond with honest reflection and maturing faith.

CHAPTER 13

Talking to Kids about God

IT'S A DAUNTING SUBJECT, but an important one — how to help children understand an invisible God, who is creator of the universe and best friend of humankind. The Catholic Church teaches that parents are the first and most important teachers of their children (see *Catechism*, 2225). As parents, we need to cultivate our own relationship with God to ensure that we are also the *best* of teachers for our children as we introduce them to their creator. Here are some tips to help your child to get to know God:

• **Pray regularly, and engage in spiritual reading.** Not just as a family, but also individually. When we have a close relationship with God, we can't help but share him with those we love. Allow your child to "catch you" praying or reading Scripture from time to time. Our actions are far more powerful than our words. Children believe in God when they see their parents acknowledging and talking to him.

- **Decorate your home with concrete symbols of your faith.** Young children especially are very concrete thinkers, and they need visible signs of God's presence in your home. Statues or pictures of Jesus are especially important. Christ is the most visible and most complete revelation of God to humankind. Consider an icon or statue of Jesus and the children (see Mt 19:13-14; Mk 10:13-14) for your child's room. This image will present the idea that God loves children and wants to be their friend.

- **With younger children, refer to God as an additional family member in your home.** When your child learns to do something new, express your pride and add: "And you know who else is proud of you? God is! We can't see him, but he can see us, and he is so happy with how you are growing — just the way he planned!"

- **As children get older, don't be afraid to tackle the difficult subjects.** On a televised press conference during Holy Week one year, Pope Benedict XVI was asked by a child from Japan how God could allow the type of suffering seen there in the wake of the earthquake and tsunami. Rather than giving a pat (and unsatisfying) answer, the pope said that this was difficult for him to understand as well. He said that one thing about which he is sure is that God makes himself very close to those who are suffering. When children and teens have difficult times, be sure to emphasize that God is sad with them and will help them through their troubles.

- **Remember that as a parent you are an icon of God to your child.** God reveals himself to us as a parent, and this makes the parent-child relationship a privileged place to learn about God. Be sure to ask for — and be open to — the grace to be a faithful sign of God's ever-present, unconditional love. In every choice you make as a parent, ask yourself, "What does this teach my child about God whom we also call Father?"

CHAPTER 14

Teaching Kids to Pray

PERHAPS THE MOST IMPORTANT LESSON we can teach our children is that God loves them. However, to truly teach our children about God's love for them, we must teach them to have conversations with God. We must teach them to pray.

There are many different ways to pray with children, but there are some general principles regarding prayer that should be understood and communicated. One is that prayer is both *talking* and *listening*. St. John Paul II once stated: "When we hold a conversation with someone, we not only speak, but we also listen. Prayer, therefore, is also listening."

Prayerful listening can include quiet time in meditation or reflection. It can also include attentiveness to God's creation, to teachers in the faith, or to holy Scripture. Some of these activities are not easy for young children. Nevertheless, children should be taught that God wants to speak to them, and that, while they might not hear him in the same way they hear family members and friends, God does make himself known.

Another important principle of prayer is that talking to God can take many forms. St. Thérèse of Lisieux taught us that even the littlest, everyday things we do can be offered as prayer to God. In this way, we can make our daily lives a constant prayer of praise and thanksgiving. Still, it is useful and necessary to take special time for more formal prayer. Prayer can, and should, occur within the flow of family life. Blessings before meals and prayers in the morning and evening are natural opportunities. Other opportunities arise in the daily circumstances of families. For example, families often pray spontaneously when a loved one is hurt or ill.

With the understanding that prayer can, and should, occur anywhere, creating a prayer space in the home can be helpful for children because it serves as a constant reminder of God's presence and our need to connect with him. A simple home altar might consist of an end table or a decorator table with a religious statue, a Bible, and a candle. You might also want to place various sacramentals, such as the Rosary, in your prayer space.

The forms of prayer we use with children should depend in part on their age and interests. Very young children — for example, toddlers and two-year-olds — will benefit a great deal from the use of pictures and statues. They can be encouraged to say "Hi" or "I love you" to Jesus depicted in a statue or painting. They can be taught to make the Sign of the Cross and taught to sing hymns. Older children should be taught both spontaneous and traditional Catholic prayers, especially those we like and use.

Traditional prayers are valuable because they enable us to pray together, in one voice, as God's people. They highlight our unity of faith and purpose. Traditional prayers also give us a repertoire from which to choose when we are not sure what to pray. Traditional prayers should be introduced gradually as children are able to understand them. We should not ask children to pray what they cannot understand, because without understanding they can't mean what they are praying. For example, very young children might learn the Sign of the Cross, then the prayer before meals and the Glory Be. A slightly older child may learn the Hail Mary and the Guardian Angel Prayer. As children get older, they are ready to understand prayers such as the Our Father and Hail, Holy Queen.

Spontaneous prayer helps us to develop the unique relationship God desires with each of us. We should teach children to both thank God for what he has done (the blessings he has given us, etc.) and praise God for who he is (all-powerful, almighty, loving, and just). Other forms of prayer include petition (making our requests known to God) and intercession (praying on behalf of others). Prayers of contrition and reconciliation are also useful for children to learn, especially when they are taught in the context of God's unconditional love ("God always forgives us when we are truly sorry").

Jesus said, "Let the children come to me, and do not hinder them; for to such belongs the kingdom of heaven" (Mt 19:14). May God richly bless your efforts to share his love with your children.

CHAPTER 15

Understanding Jesus' Crucifixion and the Meaning of Suffering

WE ALL HAVE A NATURAL TENDENCY to seek comfort and avoid suffering. This is especially true of children, who have limited delay-of-gratification skills — it's difficult for them to not have what they want right when they want it.

But suffering is a part of every life. Along with the good times, we also experience illness, hardships, disappointment, and eventually death. If our faith is to be relevant to our everyday life, it is important that a community of faith be able to give meaning to suffering and be responsive to the needs of those who are suffering.

As mentioned in an earlier chapter, once, during a question-and-answer session, Pope Benedict was asked by a young girl from Japan why people must suffer as they did in her country during the 2011 tsunami. Pope Benedict answered honestly, saying that he, too, had trouble understanding why suffering of this magnitude is present in the world. He then echoed the words of St. John Paul II, saying that one thing we can be certain about is that God is always on the side of the suffering. In the suffering Christ, we see God's solidarity with even the most painful moments of human existence.

Children's experience of God's presence often takes the same form as their interactions with friends and family, and especially with their parents. After all, God reveals himself as a parent. Therefore, all mothers and fathers are icons of God for the child. For this reason, it is important that children experience empathy from Mom and Dad, even when their suffering seems small by our standards. Reflect their feelings by saying, "I know you're frustrated that you can't play outside today," or "I'm sorry your stomach is hurting." This lets them know that you care about them, and it helps give them the strength to bear their small sufferings and build self-discipline.

Another lesson to hand on to our children is that suffering can have meaning because it is not the end of the story. The suffering of Jesus is transformed in the Resurrection. The Easter story is so very meaningful precisely because at the moment that all seemed lost, light broke forth. The one who was dead was alive again. In our human suffering, we have smaller, more everyday experiences of dying and rising as one ending gives rise to a new beginning or opportunity. We also see how suffering can be transformative in the way it can make us stronger and more determined.

Suffering also takes on an additional spiritual significance in light of our Catholic faith. God does not will suffering, but he can miraculously make good come from bad circumstances, just as he brought salvation from the suffering of Jesus. The

Church, as the Body of Christ, continues this redemptive work as we allow God to mysteriously bring spiritual good from our own experiences of suffering. St. Paul refers to this in Colossians 1:24 as he points out that through offering our sufferings for the sake of others we are joined to Christ's redemptive work. This is what Catholic parents and grandparents of prior generations meant when they said, "Offer it up!" Offering our sufferings for the good of others (and especially for the holy souls in purgatory) can be a beautiful and meaningful thing, but a simple "offer it up" spoken without empathy can sometimes be confusing for a child.

The light of hope shines brightest against the darkness of sorrow. For it is at this time that we must depend most fully on hope in order to claim the joy that is ours. God is with us, and all darkness, all mourning, every sorrow will one day disappear in the light of Christ.

Talking with Kids about Jesus' Death

The mystery of Jesus' death and resurrection is central to our faith. Kids who are raised Catholic need to be (and will be) exposed to the Cross in some way from the very beginning of their lives. Some children get over-focused on the morbid aspects of the crucifixion story if they get hit with too much detail at too early an age. When children are young, avoid too much blood and violence in images/films depicting the Crucifixion.

Children can experience the Stations of the Cross at most ages, as long as they have some developmentally appropriate way to experience this devotion — for example, a child's guidebook. It's important to keep the Resurrection in mind and foreshadow this event as we are talking with kids about Jesus' death. We should continually reassure them that this was not the end of the story.

Young children will have great difficulty with the idea of Jesus dying for our sins. When kids ask why Jesus had to die, admit that this is difficult to understand, but also say that he loved us so much and wanted so much to help us know God that he came to earth even though he knew he would be killed.

CHAPTER 16

Daughters and Sons of God through Baptism

THROUGH BAPTISM, WE ARE FREED from original sin, we receive the gift of the Holy Spirit (which will be renewed and
strengthened in confirmation), and we become adopted sons
and daughters of God. This bestows upon us great responsibility and great dignity. Our place in the Christian community,
our relationship with Christ, and God's plan for our lives are all
built upon the foundation of our baptism. We should work to
help children understand this important sacrament and their
unique status as daughters and sons of God. This will happen
little by little as children are developmentally able to understand.

Parents can help children understand their baptism in a
number of ways. One is to help them see what baptism looks
like by demonstrating with a baby doll and ordinary water. Another is to look at pictures and/or videos of their child's baptism
and discuss what is happening in the pictures. It may also be

helpful for parents to share their own memories of that special day.

Visiting the baptismal font and looking at the Paschal candle in the church can offer an additional opportunity to discuss the visible signs of the sacrament. Although young children are not likely to understand how these visible things signify spiritual realities, learning about the form and physical signs can set the stage for unfolding understanding over time.

It is important to convey the reality of our place in God's family. We should teach that we are a close community and care for one another, and that each person in your family has great value. For example, when encouraging children to take turns, you might say, "Members of God's family share with one another." Look for opportunities for children to help one another with tasks, and prompt them to do so. Mention that in God's family we help one another. Take time to talk with each child individually, learning about their interests and pointing out their talents and gifts.

Finally, point out the similarities between Jesus' life and the lives of the children in the family. For example, Jesus was once a little child. Jesus had parents. Jesus helped his mother and father. Jesus talked to God the Father. Jesus played with other children. This identification with Jesus will lay the groundwork for the primary call of baptism — to be a follower of Christ, imitating him in word and deed, and making him present in visible ways in our daily lives.

Chapter 17

Reconciliation — the Good, the Bad, and the Merciful

FOR THE FIRST FEW YEARS OF LIFE, a child's idea of right and wrong is highly dependent on consequences. Kids learn very early that some actions lead to good things, while others get them into trouble. But this type of moral reasoning is highly subjective, dependent on who is watching and what situation they find themselves in. It is also subjective in the sense that preschoolers sometimes seem to think that saying something will make it happen (or "un-happen," as in, "I didn't take any cookies from the cookie jar!").

Over time, children become more able to understand cause and effect, and they realize that most things in this world work according to rules. Around age six or seven, children show the beginnings of "concrete operational" thinking. This is a rule-focused type of thinking in which kids use their knowledge of cause and effect to construct a worldview. They tend to be very concerned about what the rules are in various places and situations, and are quick to tattle on others who are not following the rules! Second grade is an ideal time, then, to begin a conversation with children about God's rules for living, especially the Ten Commandments. But when kids learn God's commandments, they simultaneously begin to realize that they have broken some of the rules (and continue to do so at times). We call this failure to follow God's guidelines "sin." It's essential, then, at this stage of life, that we also offer children an opportunity to be assured of God's unconditional love and to experience his forgiveness. Therefore, this is often the time that children first celebrate the Sacrament of Reconciliation.

In a culture that is quite preoccupied with nurturing healthy self-esteem, we might sometimes be reluctant to have much discussion of sin with young children. However, psychological research tells us that what is most important to our psychological functioning and healthy living is not our self-esteem (our feelings about ourselves in isolation), but our self-efficacy (our sense of what it is possible for us to do, our feeling that we can shape our lives and do good things). In fact, it may be very possible for a person to feel great about himself or herself and still be very selfish and ungodly. It's important for us, at the beginning of our lives, to have a sense of what God has planned for us — what he made us for. Children cannot rise to standards we do not set.

Incidentally, a focus on whom God created us to be, how we are meant to live, is not negative at all, but hopeful. We are made to love, to give of ourselves, and to do good in the world. This is a positive message, and we feel good about ourselves in response to it. But in order to be all we were made to be, we must also be realistic about where we are, and how we need to grow.

We feel sorry for the wrong we have done (and the good things we didn't do), but this sorrow is balanced by our experience of God's mercy and forgiveness.

The following are some practical tips for helping your child understand sin, forgiveness, and the beauty of the Sacrament of Reconciliation:

- **Look for natural opportunities to discuss God's rules, sin, and forgiveness** in the context of family life. The most important part of learning right and wrong is understanding how to apply it to our lives in practical ways. This will become most evident in our relationships with others (parents, siblings, etc.). Practice forgiveness and reconciliation in difficult family situations.

- **Reflect on your own attitudes toward sin and forgiveness**, and your experiences of the sacrament. Sometimes we can communicate big things to our children in subtle ways. Does your child see you being realistic about your shortcomings and apologizing when you need to? Do you make the celebration of the Sacrament of Reconciliation a regular practice? Or do you have some residual fears about or negative attitudes toward confession?

- **Help your child understand the difference between a sin and an accident.** We sin when we *choose* to do wrong. Make an extra effort to be patient with your child's mistakes or accidents, but hold him or her responsible for wrong choices. You might even provide some ways to help your children make up for negative behaviors — for example, doing something nice for a sibling they have wronged.

- **Attend a communal reconciliation service as a family.** These are hosted by many parishes during Advent and Lent. This helps children become more comfortable with the sacrament, and often allows them to see others (such as Mom or Dad) celebrating it. Emphasize that the sacrament is not a punishment but is a way to experience God's mercy and forgiveness. It is both a reminder and an experience of the reality that "God loves us no matter what."

- **Remember that morality is more about what we do than behaviors we avoid.** Make an effort as a family to practice good deeds at home and in the community.

COMING BACK TO THE SACRAMENT OF RECONCILIATION

Some parents are nervous about going to confession if it has been some time since they celebrated the sacrament. Here are a few tips for adults who are feeling anxious:

- Remember that reconciliation is a reminder of God's unconditional love. Read Jesus' parable of the prodigal son in Scripture (see Lk 15:11-32). Jesus told this story to teach us what God is like. He is always ready to welcome and forgive.

- Pray to the Holy Spirit, asking for guidance about what to confess. Don't become stressed by trying to remember every occasion of sin since your last confession. Rather, focus on serious sins and/or any recurrent struggles. If you have quite a bit to discuss, you might wish to make an appointment with the priest so that you don't feel rushed.

- Find a simple guide to confession, and feel free to take it with you if you need a "cheat sheet." You can also let the priest know that it has been awhile since you celebrated the sacrament, so that he can help you through it. You need not feel embarrassed. Most priests are delighted to see someone return to the sacrament after some time.

QUESTIONS FOR REFLECTION
ON PART THREE

In what stage of faith development might your son or daughter be? What can you do to help him or her continue to form a relationship with Jesus and his Church?

~

What conversations have you had with your child about God? What are some concrete ways in which you show your child who God is to you?

~

How and when do you pray together as a family? What are some additional ways to integrate prayer into your family life?

~

What are some ways you have suffered as a family? How have you felt God's presence at those times?

~

When is your child's baptismal anniversary? How can your family celebrate this special day each year?

~

How does your child understand sin and reconciliation? How can your family more fully experience and appreciate the Sacrament of Penance?

A Parent's Prayer

Dear God, teaching my child about you can sometimes be a daunting task, but I know that you have made me my child's first and most important teacher of the Faith. Help me to show my child who you are through my actions and my words. Amen.

PART FOUR

RAISING CHILDREN OF VIRTUE

CHAPTER 18

Forgiveness — It's a Family Affair

FORGIVENESS IS VITAL TO THE CHRISTIAN LIFE, and there is no more important place to practice forgiveness than in the family. Why? Because the family is the *school of charity* — it is where we first learn to love others. The *Catechism of the Catholic Church* calls the family the *domestic church*: the place where the Christian community is formed (see 1655-1658).

Forgiveness is at the heart of Jesus' teaching. He says that if we forgive others, God will also forgive us (see Mt 6:14-15). He puts no limits on this, commanding us to forgive "seventy times seven" times (Mt 18:21-22).

Hurts do occur in families — even healthy families. The most common causes of conflict between spouses include disagreements over finances, problems in the area of sexuality or intimacy, and conflicts over rules and limits for children. Parent-child conflict may center on chores, homework, schedule or time pressures, wants versus needs, and differing ideas about age-appropriate freedoms. Sibling conflict often centers on shared space, taking turns with shared possessions, and teasing that turns ugly.

AN OUNCE OF PREVENTION

Of course, the best way to manage such conflicts is to prevent as much as possible in the first place. In doing so, we can shorten the list of offenses that need to be forgiven. For spouses, this means being proactive about budgeting and sticking to an agreed-upon family budget, being open about intimacy needs and preferences, and taking time to be with one another.

For parents and kids, minimizing conflict means first paying attention to the quality of the parent-child relationship. Is enough time being spent building a relationship in a positive way, or are parent-child interactions more about setting rules and policing? We tend to want to please people we like. Invest in the parent-child relationship by taking some low-key time to do something together that your child enjoys. Also, be consistent about limits, and make sure consequences are directly related to the offenses. Imposed, contrived punishments can make a child resentful.

Sibling conflict can be reduced and prevented through organized turn-taking — for example, using a kitchen timer to determine when it's time to take turns on the computer. Parents can act as "coaches" or interpreters in conflicts between siblings. Instead of solving the problem yourself, act as an intermediary and ask each child to express his or her feelings to the other and to generate possible solutions. Quality individual time with each child that capitalizes on the child's unique interests can also help to temper feelings of sibling rivalry.

WHEN HURTS DO OCCUR

While we can minimize family conflict, we can't eliminate it. Hurts will occur; this is the nature of human relationships. When this happens, recognizing and using some basic steps toward reconciliation can be helpful. For those who have been hurt, recalling and expressing the hurt is the first step toward reconciliation. We can't heal what we don't feel. Some infractions may be so small that we can brush them aside and forget them. But anything that is important enough to remember is important enough to talk about. Otherwise, we may later be dealing with a long list of grudges instead of just one issue. Second, it's important that we try to imagine ourselves in the other person's shoes and determine why he or she might have acted in a hurtful way. We would assume that in most families people don't set out to be hurtful to one another. Rather, hurtful actions arise in a particular circumstance. What made this person feel that it was okay to say or do this? If we don't know, we may need to ask. Third, make a decision to work toward reconciliation. Fourth, offer forgiveness, recognizing that offering forgiveness does not mean all is forgotten, but that it says you are willing to work toward trust again.

When we recognize that we have been hurtful, there are also important steps we can take toward reconciliation. First, we should think through the situation carefully, and try to imagine what it must have been like for the other person. How did he or she interpret our actions, and how could that have felt? Realize that seeking reconciliation means making yourself vulnerable and admitting you were wrong, even if you feel the other person didn't handle it well either. Tell the other person what you now understand about how he or she felt, and make a commitment to avoid being hurtful in the future. Finally, realize that forgiveness is a choice, but trust is not. While the other person may forgive you, it may take some time for trust to be reestablished. Be patient with this process.

PRACTICING FORGIVENESS IN YOUR FAMILY

- **Be sure to model forgiveness for your children** — both inside and outside the home. Let them see you working things out with others. While it generally isn't good for kids to be exposed to all the emotion and adult issues inherent in parental conflict, parents who never have any conflict in front of their children may actually be doing them a disservice. That's because the children miss important examples of effective problem solving (and they may also grow up to think that a good relationship means never arguing at all). Don't argue in front of your kids about rules for their behavior, adult issues such as sexuality, or very emotional issues that are likely to lead to a heated exchange. In the smaller issues, let them see you express different points of view and arrive at a compromise.

- **Practice "penance" in the home**. When hurts have occurred between family members, encourage children to do something to help repair the relationship. For example, the big brother who let playful teasing progress to bullying may be required to do something extra nice for the sibling he offended.

- **Eat meals together as a family** on a regular basis without distractions, such as television. Research has shown that families who eat together around a table on a regular basis communicate better and have less conflict.

- **Celebrate the Sacrament of Reconciliation as a family**. Make it a practice to go together to celebrate reconciliation on a regular basis. While each family member will talk individually with the priest, family issues will undoubtedly be discussed. It's important for kids to see that their parents also need God's forgiveness. Celebrating the sacrament also allows us to partake of God's grace as we build a home of love and reconciliation.

CHAPTER 19

Teaching Kids about Responsibility

THE *CATECHISM OF THE CATHOLIC CHURCH* DESCRIBES the family as "a communion of persons, a sign and image of the communion of the Father and the Son in the Holy Spirit" (2205). In other words, our families are called to be a sign of the unity and collaboration of the persons of the Blessed Trinity. Just as the Father, Son, and Spirit work in concert to bring about God's plan of salvation, families work together for the good of one another.

This all sounds great in theory, but in practice parents do most of the work, don't they? In some ways, this is appropriate, because the parent-child relationship, while one of mutual love, is not entirely reciprocal. Kids come to us completely dependent on us to give them what they need. But over time, kids can and *should* learn to do some things for themselves, including work that benefits the whole family. This is an important part of becoming self-giving persons who model the perfect self-gift of

Jesus Christ. Here are a few guidelines for teaching children to take some responsibility for family work:

- Explain that "**in families, we work together.**" Help your child understand that because he or she benefits from the life and resources of the family, it's reasonable for him or her to contribute in some way.

- **Consider allowing kids to decide together** with you which tasks they will help complete. Make a list of the jobs to be done and divide the responsibilities in a family discussion. (This also helps kids to see *how much* you do for them, some of which they may not notice.)

- **Pay attention to developmental needs**. Realize that the younger the child, the less he or she is able to focus for long periods of time. Also, be cautious about giving children responsibilities that should be reserved for adults. Take care when assigning tasks that include responsibility for younger siblings. Avoid giving them tasks that could pose a safety risk if not done correctly — for example, cooking dinner or cleaning with chemicals.

- **Give clear and concise directions**. Most younger children can only remember one or two step directions. More complicated tasks might require more supervision.

- When possible, **work together on tasks**. For example, if the dishes need to be done, you might do the scrubbing while one child rinses and another dries or puts dishes away. This type of collaboration helps tasks get done faster and models the larger message that families need to work together. Plus, there's the added benefit of an opportunity for parent-child interaction. Some kids talk more openly with adults when they are doing something else with their hands. To take the best advantage of this, make sure televisions and other distractions are turned off.

Made in God's image, we are created to live and work in relationship with one another. In the family, and in the Church, we are at our best when we all work together.

CHAPTER 20

Coaching Kids to Be Good Winners

MANY LESSONS ABOUT LIFE can be learned through sports, including teamwork, perseverance toward a goal, and conflict resolution. One thing we often try to teach is good sportsmanship. When our children lose a game, or when the other team scores, we remind them to be polite and courteous. We want them to learn from mistakes and congratulate others. Another important lesson — one that may be overlooked at times — is how to be a good winner.

We've all been around people who succeed and want everyone to know about it. They seem to think they are better than everyone else, or they need continuous affirmation from others. They may flaunt their victories, or throw them in others' faces. Then, when others have had all they can stand, those same people ask, "Why does everybody hate me?"

While we want children to feel good about their successes,

we don't want them to become impossible to live with. Patience and self-control, characteristics of humility, are fruits of the Holy Spirit (see Gal 5:22-23). How can we help children see victories in the appropriate light and become "good winners"? Here are a few tips:

- **Remind them that all we have comes from God**. We are sons and daughters of our creator, and that's something to feel good about. But, it can also keep us humble. We need to remember that God gives us our talents and abilities — even those potentials we have fostered through hard work. And God gives us our talents for a purpose — not so we can brag about them to others, but so we can glorify him. Encourage your child to thank God for his or her victories and to ask for guidance about how to bring glory to God through this ability.

- **Ask your child to name the strengths of his or her "opponents."** A good winner congratulates others on a game played well. Encourage your child to note what others do well and to offer them genuine compliments — for example, "Your great pitching really challenged us on the field today." Explain to your child that while he or she may be very excited about winning, a child who lost may be feeling sad. Ask your child to give some encouragement to that child, which also shows he or she can win with grace.

- **Avoid focusing too much on your child's accomplishments.** Parents who talk nonstop about how their child is doing are not modeling humility. It's okay to feel proud, and even to show it in front of your child, but don't overdo it. Show genuine interest in the families of others and your child will learn to follow your example.

- **Encourage your child to celebrate and then move on.** It's never attractive to see a middle-aged person still basking in the glory of his high school football days. A victory is cause for celebration, but it doesn't mean we have arrived. Ask your child where God is calling him or her to grow next. What goal would your child like to set for his or her next accomplishment? Where could he or she improve and do even better next time?

- **Remind your child that every member of the team counts in a special way.** Some kids get more playing time than others. It is important to learn that, whether you're the "star" player or on the backup squad, God has given each of us our own unique talents and gifts.

Winning isn't everything, but it sure is nice once in a while. May all your child's victories be sweet — both for your child and for others.

Five Ways to
Nurture Fortitude

FORTITUDE IS THE MORAL VIRTUE that allows us to persevere in the face of struggles and obstacles in pursuit of something good. One of the cardinal virtues, fortitude, helps us to be the people God made us to be, to finish the work to which he has called us, and to hold on to our faith in the face of persecution. Here are five ways parents can nurture the virtue of fortitude in their children:

1. **Promote self-efficacy.** Research on achievement tells us that success is highly correlated with measures of ability, but it is even more closely related to self-efficacy, the belief that we *can* do something. Tell your child that you know he or she can do it, and talk about why. You might mention other times he or she prevailed in the face of a struggle, or a particular talent that makes your child suited to the task.

2. **Don't let them give up too soon.** It's not always easy to do the right thing. In a culture of immediate gratification, we sometimes inadvertently send the message that anything that takes too much effort isn't worth trying (or just isn't meant to be). However, many of the best things in life take work, and some great things come only after real struggle. When kids want to give up, encourage them to go just a little further and think about it again. For example, if your daughter wants to quit piano or dance because it's feeling too difficult, encourage her to hang in there until the next recital. Then she can rethink whether she wants to continue. Tell her you will let the decision be hers at that point, as long as you see genuine effort between now and then. This can also teach children important lessons about following through with commitments.

3. **Model perseverance.** When you are working on something difficult, allow your child to see you persevering in the face of struggle. Help your child see what it means to keep going even when things are difficult.

4. **Work with your child.** The child development theorist Lev Vygotsky emphasized the role parents play in helping children learn new tasks by giving them just the right amount of help they need, and then easing back from that help as they learn to do things on their own. If you believe your child might be in over his or her head, do what you can to share some of the work, so he or she can follow through to the end. Try to do only as much as you are certain he or

she can't do alone. That might mean guiding with relevant questions, pitching in here and there, or giving a framework of steps that can guide your child through the task.

5. **Emphasize the role of grace.** God doesn't call people to things they can't do. But, we see many examples in Scripture of God calling people to do things they can't do *on their own*. Encourage your child to talk to God about his or her struggles, and to depend on God's grace to help them keep going. St. Paul, who faced many obstacles and much persecution in his ministry said, "I can do all things in him who strengthens me" (Phil 4:13).

CHAPTER 22

Seven Secrets of Successful, Self-Giving Children

ASK PARENTS ABOUT THEIR HOPES AND DREAMS for their children, and you're likely to get a variety of responses, which will include academic achievement, occupational success, fulfilling relationships, and so on. Investing in children's future success is a major task of parenthood, and we do many different things to accomplish it, including buying educational toys, involving kids in sports and other extracurricular activities, hiring tutors, and having important talks about responsibility.

Some parents seem to push so hard that we call them "stage parents." We worry about the stress they may be placing on their children and the highly competitive environment they help to cultivate. At the same time, children rarely rise to their potential without some encouragement, and we recognize that it often takes a measure of pressure to foster self-discipline.

So where is the line between "pushover" and "pushy"? How do we know how much to drive our children without driving them (and us) crazy? How do we define "success"? In a purely secular sense, being successful often means beating out the competition, or rising to the top. Our Catholic faith defines success differently. Jesus said, "He who is greatest among you shall be your servant" (Mt 23:11). As Jesus gave completely of himself, we are called to give of ourselves to others. Blessed Mother Teresa of Calcutta said, "God didn't call us to be successful; he called us to be faithful."

Self-giving takes many forms based on our own talents and personalities. Each of us has unique, God-given gifts that we are called to share with others. Here are some tips for helping young children find and follow God's plan for their lives, and in so doing achieve true success:

1. **Starting when they are young, tell your children that God has a plan for their lives.** Pray with them that they will discover this plan and live it.

2. **Nurture a love for and knowledge of sacred Scripture.** Applying God's revelation in Scripture to our own personal circumstances can be one starting point for discerning his will in our lives.

3. **Help your children stay connected with the Christian community** so there will be other people in their lives who will encourage and help point the way to God's plan. Ways to get to know others and stay connected may include parish family events, parish religious education, and participation in youth groups.

4. **Invest in particular talents and interests shown by your child**. Make sure he or she has the resources to bring a talent to its full potential, but be careful about pushing too far. Pursuing a very restricted range of activities can sometimes lead to burnout.

5. **While you are nurturing your child's interest in a particular area, be sure to encourage him or her to engage in other activities as well.** While children and teens have some ideas about what interests them, there are many things they haven't yet tried, and they are not ready to make clear decisions about what they will do for the rest of their lives.

6. **Brainstorm with your children about ways to "give back" to others**. It can sometimes take a little creativity, but talents are meant to be shared. Where there is a gift or strength, there is also an opportunity for giving.

7. **Realize that very few individuals become "superstars."** The chances that the son who enjoys football will win a college scholarship or play in the NFL are very slim, but he may find a great deal of fulfillment in coaching sports at the local middle school. On the other hand, don't tell him he'll *never* grow up to play in the NFL. Some do!

CHAPTER 23

Ten Commandments of
Talking to Kids about Sexuality

RESEARCH TELLS US that a majority of parents believe they *should* talk with their children about sex, but many are uncomfortable doing so. Still, kids are — and should be — looking to their parents for information about sexuality. Several studies suggest that teens prefer to get this information from their parents. These studies state that their parents are the single biggest influence in their decision-making about sexual issues. In today's sexually charged culture, it's more important than ever that parents offer guidance on making right choices. Here are "ten commandments" of talking to your children about sex:

1. **Foster a close parent-child relationship.** Teens who are connected to their parents are less likely to engage in risky sexual behavior. Your guidance about sex and other sensitive issues will be most credible to your teen if that guidance

is given within the context of a warm, loving relationship. That means spending quality time with your teen and getting to know his or her interests.

2. **Start early.** Waiting well into the teenage years to talk about sex may be too late. Research indicates that the average age of first exposure to pornography is between eight and eleven years old. One study by the Kaiser Family Foundation said that 33 percent of ten- to eleven-year-olds said that the pressure to engage in sexual activity is a "big problem" for them. In addition to the danger that your child may face pressure to engage in sexual activity sooner than you expected, waiting too long to address sexual issues may make talking with your child more difficult.

3. **Provide accurate, developmentally appropriate information**. Children are ready to learn about various aspects of sexuality at different ages. While very young — for example, preschool age — children may need to know only the accurate names of their private parts and that these parts are off-limits to others. Children in elementary school should be educated about the physical changes of puberty well before they begin to develop sexually. As you offer information about sexuality, be sure the information you are providing is accurate. Consult trusted resources, and if you do not know the answer to one of your child's questions, don't be afraid to admit it. Saying, "I don't know," and then researching the answer using reliable resources is much better than giving misinformation.

4. **Place information about sexuality in the context of faith, morality, and relationships.** Human beings are more than biological urges, drives, and processes. Parent-teen discussion about sex should reflect this. Talk about how our Catholic faith informs our decisions about sexual behavior. Discuss your personal values regarding sexual issues. Also, discuss the purpose and role of sex in the larger context of relationships.

5. **Use everyday opportunities to discuss sexual issues.** Parents can use songs on the radio, television commercials, or scenes from movies as discussion starters. Looking for everyday opportunities to talk about sex will also help conversations between you and your child feel less "forced." In contrast, having "the big talk" on just one occasion may feel unnatural. It may also do the child a disservice because he or she needs to talk with you more than once over these years of rapid growth and maturity.

6. **Provide clear guidance and limits.** Our children cannot rise to standards that we do not set. Make no apologies for presenting chastity as the best and only choice until marriage. Not only is this what is taught by the Church, it is scientifically accurate as well. Abstinence from sexual activity is the only 100 percent sure way to prevent pregnancy and sexually transmitted infections.

7. **Provide medical reasons in addition to moral reasons for abstaining from sexual activity.** Let your teen know that

there are serious medical risks involved if he or she engages in sexual behavior. Not only can this be life-saving information, it illustrates how God's laws serve to protect our well-being in very practical ways. One good resource for parents (though not a Catholic one) is the Medical Institute for Sexual Health (medinstitute.org). The Medical Institute for Sexual Health supports the involvement of parents in sexuality education and promotes abstinence education for teens.

8. **Frame the conversation in terms of goals.** Discuss the positives your child wants in his or her life and what will lead to those goals. A collaborative study between the University of Pennsylvania and the University of Waterloo in Canada showed that abstinence education is the most effective deterrent to early sexual activity provided that it is framed in terms of positive goals — not only risks. Fear-based tactics alone often do not work, because teens tend to think they will be the exceptions to the rule.

9. **Be aware of other influences that may come between you and your child on sexuality issues.** Parents should find out what sexuality education programs are offered in their child's school and evaluate how the messages children receive there fit with the values they wish to promote. If there is a conflict, voice concerns to school personnel and, if necessary, to the local school board. Other potentially dangerous influences include pressure from peers and media messages. Keep an open dialogue with your child regard-

ing these influences. While you often cannot control every message your child hears about sex, you should weigh in with your own guidance.

10. **Ask God to guide you and your child.** Pray that the Holy Spirit will assist your child in making important decisions about relationships and sexual behavior. Ask the Holy Spirit to guide you as you help to form your child's moral decision-making. We can't always be with our children, but God will. Thank him for his loving care, and ask the heavenly Father for the grace to be the parent your child needs.

QUESTIONS FOR REFLECTION ON PART FOUR

Who do you need to forgive right now? From whom do you need to ask forgiveness?

~

In what ways have you taught your child about responsibility? In what ways is he or she responsible? Where does responsibility need to grow before additional freedoms are given?

~

Is your child a "good winner"? How have you encouraged him or her to be a good sport?

~

How does your child show determination and fortitude? In what areas can you assist him or her in exerting more effort or patience?

~

How do you define "success"? How are being successful and being self-giving related in the Christian life?

~

How are you addressing the area of sexuality with your child? Are you waiting for one "big talk," or are you taking advantage of natural opportunities to shape his or her behavior?

A Parent's Prayer

*Dear God, help me in my vocation of raising a virtuous child.
Give me, first and foremost, the grace to be a good example.
Give me wisdom to know the ways in which my child needs to
grow and the courage to have even the difficult conversations
that will help my child on this path. Amen.*

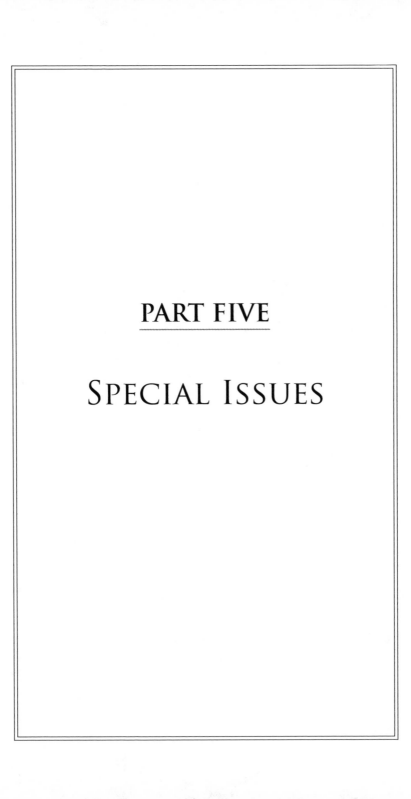

PART FIVE

SPECIAL ISSUES

CHAPTER 24

Moving from Fear to Courage and Confidence

THE PHRASE "DO NOT BE AFRAID," or something close to it, appears in the Bible over three hundred times. That makes the admonition "not to fear" God's most frequent message to us in Scripture. Perhaps this is because God knew we would need to hear it so many times, for fear is one of our earliest companions on the journey of life. Even in infants, we see fear of new environments, persons, and things.

Every autumn brings the beginning of a new school year. With new beginnings come new fears — for parents and children. Fears of starting school for the first time and separating from Mom or Dad, fears of beginning middle school or high school, fears of leaving home for college.

Parents may also fear for their children at these times of transitions, or have related fears of their own. Will we really be able to make ends meet as we choose a Catholic school for our child? Will going back to work now that the kids are in school result in success or failure for me or for my children?

Yet, God never calls us to something we can't handle. His plans for us don't include failure. Jeremiah 29:11 says, "For I know the plans I have for you, says the Lord, plans for welfare and not for evil, to give you a future and a hope." How can we follow God's word to "be not afraid"? How can we help our children be confident in God's plans for them? Here are a few steps for helping families move from fear to confidence and courage:

- **Call on God, and trust that God is with you.** The passage from Jeremiah referenced above continues with, "Then you will call upon me and come and pray to me, and I will hear you. You will seek me and find me with all your heart" (vv. 12-13). A good portion of Jesus' Sermon on the Mount (see Mt 5:1—7:29) is devoted to trusting that God is a good Father, and that we have no need to worry. Near the end, Jesus asks, "Which one of you would hand his son a stone when he asks for a loaf of bread, or a snake when he asks for a fish? If you then, who are wicked, know how to give good gifts to your children, how much more will your heavenly Father give good things to those who ask him" (Mt 7:9-11, New American Bible).

- **Use effective, God-given coping techniques.** Science tells us that when we are fearful, our bodies often go into an instinctual "fight or flight" response. In other words, our brains, believing we truly are in danger, send a rush of adrenaline that mobilizes our whole body for escape or conflict. Our heart rate increases, our muscles tense, and much of our brain activity moves from the logical, reasoning areas to the parts of the nervous system associated with running or fighting. When this happens, we often don't do our best thinking. But, we can reverse this process by taking deep breaths, relaxing our muscles, and using logical thoughts to help combat our fearful ones. Sometimes we fear failure or new experiences with only a very fuzzy idea of what can happen. Very few choices involve the possibility of mortal danger or the end of the world. It may be helpful for us (or our children) to pause and consider, "What's the worst that could really happen?" In a related vein, if we are anxious because we *are* considering the worst-case scenario, we might ask ourselves, "Is that *likely* to happen?" For example, a common fear of school-age children is that their parents will die. In my own counseling practice, when kids verbalize this fear, I sometimes ask, "Has that happened to a lot of your friends?" The answer, inevitably, is "no." I then follow this up by saying: "It sounds like parents don't usually die when their children are your age. Maybe you don't need to be so worried about that."

- **Set a good example.** One of the leading causes of child anxiety is anxiety in parents. Let your child see you facing new situations with confidence and he or she will feel more confident and capable as well.

- **Go forward in courage.** If God tells us so many times not to be afraid, he does not want us to let fear decide things for us. Research in psychology tells us that anxiety is strengthened when we let ourselves, or our children, escape situations out of fear. Fear dissipates considerably when we face the feared situation head-on and see that it is not as bad as we might have imagined. When your children are fearful, don't give them a lot of extra help. That may inadvertently send the signal that they *can't* handle something. Instead, give confident reassurance that you know they are capable and an extra little nudge, if necessary, to do what you believe they can do.

"But I Didn't Do It!"

MANY PARENTS FACE THE SAME DILEMMA. A teacher, coach, or other adult reports that their children have misbehaved, even giving details about the incident. But, when the children are confronted about it, they sweetly and innocently explain that the adult must be mistaken. They claim they did no such thing. Or perhaps the misbehavior occurs at home. Cookies mysteriously disappear from the cookie jar, or something turns up broken. Your child claims to know nothing about it. Sound familiar? Here are a few tips for handling those times when you don't get the whole story:

- **Recognize when lying is a developmental issue.** When children are about three or four years old, their language skills get ahead of their logic and reasoning skills. During this stage, called "preoperational thinking," they might tell us what they *wish* were true, rather than the cold, hard facts. They think that reality might be changed by their words. In this instance, it's sometimes helpful to say, for example, "You *wish* you hadn't hit your brother, because you know you're not supposed to, but you *did*." Of course, consequences for misbehavior still apply because children this age are working on mastering the idea that the world works according to rules. They need to learn that you don't change what happened by claiming it didn't.

- **Determine who has the most to gain by lying.** It is a parent's job to be his or her child's No. 1 advocate, and many parents will rush to defend their child if they believe he or she has been wronged. But in situations in which an adult claims to have actually seen children misbehaving, or when other objective evidence exists, we might need to suspend our defensive instincts. Children know that good parents will protect their children. Sometimes they rely on this to get out of trouble. Of course, we wouldn't always believe an adult's word over a child's, but in situations like this, it's the child who has the most to gain by lying. It is helpful to explain this to our children when they express surprise that we don't believe the story they are telling us. This is an especially effective approach for children ages seven to twelve who tend to be very concrete thinkers.

- **Do a little surveillance.** You might wish to watch your children at times when they don't know you are looking, both at home and at other places. If you see them doing something they shouldn't, don't talk about it right away. Instead, bring it up later, saying you *know* what happened. This will send the message that they won't always know when you are looking, so they should be on their best behavior even when they think you don't see them. This is especially true for younger children, who might even believe Mom and Dad have a "sixth sense" about their behavior! Be judicious in your use of this technique for adolescents, however. While teens don't have an absolute right to privacy, their self-consciousness makes them vulnerable to misperceiving and overreacting to parental spying.

- **Frame the matter in terms of trust.** As parents, we are sometimes inclined to stretch the limits of credibility because we don't want to believe our children would actually look us in the eyes and lie. That's because trust is at the heart of close relationships. When our children lie to us, they are, at some level, telling us that we can't trust them — and that *they* don't trust *us* with the truth. You can say, "I want us to be close, but we can't be as close as we should be if we can't trust each other." When kids insist they are being accused of something they didn't do, and no adult actually saw what happened, encourage them to consider why the accusation sounds credible. You might ask, "Why do you think I *believe* you might have done this?" or "Why do you think your teacher *believes* that you did it?" Perhaps the child has worn down trust by engaging in similar behaviors in the past. If so, explain that trust can take a long time to build back up again, and the only way to do this is to be trustworthy over a period of time. Encourage your children to accept the consequences of this lack of trust (even if they continue to maintain their innocence) and to work to rebuild trust by consistently doing the right thing in a visible way. This approach works well with children who are school age and above, including teens, for whom mutual trust is often very important.

CHAPTER 26

Navigating Conflicts with Peers

LEARNING HOW TO SOLVE PROBLEMS WITH PEERS is essential to living a happy, successful life. God created each of us to be unique and un-repeatable. As such, we sometimes have different ideas, opinions, and preferences. This naturally leads to conflict at times, even with our closest friends and family members. Parents can help kids learn how to work through these conflicts in healthy and productive ways. Here are four things parents can do to help kids grow in this area:

1. **Be a good example**. Model healthy conflict resolution, both within and outside the home. You've heard it said that parents shouldn't argue in front of their children. This is true if the disagreement is over a parenting issue or the argument is so heated that there is yelling or strong emotions. However, children can benefit from seeing Mom and Dad work through small differences in a calm, respectful way. Outside the home, parents can set an example by what they do (and

don't do) with their own peers. Model healthy assertiveness with others. Avoid the two extremes of either withdrawing and not speaking about conflict or yelling and losing your temper.

2. **Don't get too involved**. It almost never goes well when parents get too involved in their children's conflicts with peers. Talking to the peer yourself, confronting the other child's parents, or offering a solution too quickly can turn the situation into a missed opportunity for the child to learn new skills. It can also make things worse if the child is perceived as a tattletale, or if your efforts are misunderstood. A better approach is to serve as a problem-solving consultant. Be a resource to your child. Allow him or her to "check-in" with you about what's going on, and assist your child in thinking through possible solutions.

3. **Help your child use problem-solving steps.** Try the 1-2-3-check method of problem solving: 1) What is the problem? 2) What are my choices? 3) Take the best action. 4) Check and see: How did it work? Talk through these steps with your child, away from the situation itself. Imagine that you are a coach on the sidelines. Then, send your child back into the game after helping him or her formulate a strategy. Don't give solutions too quickly, but provide suggestions if your child gets stuck.

4. **Encourage your child to forgive others and ask forgiveness when appropriate.** Forgiveness is an important part of

our Catholic faith. Jesus said that if we forgive others, God will also forgive us (see Mt 6:14-15). Provided that your child's peer is not chronically disrespectful of your child, teach your child how to repair the relationship and move forward. This might mean accepting someone else's apology. It might mean learning to say "I'm sorry" as well. It might also mean a concrete action to demonstrate a desire to reconcile.

Most close relationships have occasional rough patches or miscommunications, which is part of being human. Learning to solve problems with others will give your child a solid foundation for future relationships — skills he or she can use for a lifetime.

CHAPTER 27

Kids and the News

WE ARE A NEWS-HUNGRY CULTURE and find updates of current events readily available on cable television and the Internet. This presents parents with a dilemma. How much news is too much for our children? We don't want our children to be naive, and we can't shelter them from everything. But, the frequent doses of violence portrayed on the news can surely be too much. What's a parent to do?

According to U.S. Surgeon General reports, the percentage of children in the United States who currently have anxiety disorders has risen from 8 percent to 13 percent in the years since 2001. While researchers have not fully accounted for this disturbing trend, the news in a post-9/11 world has certainly become not only more prolific, but also much more scary. Common fears shared by children at the elementary school age include being kidnapped, robbed, or murdered. Even though the odds of becoming a victim of violent crime in the United States have actually decreased over the past decade, the constant barrage of accounts of violent crimes can lead children (and some adults) to believe these events are more common than they actually are. We should let kids be kids, but not be completely ignorant of current events or the dangers of the outside world. Here is an age-by-age guide for monitoring your child's exposure to the news:

AGES 0-6: NO NEWS IS GOOD NEWS

Children below the age of seven have trouble understanding much of what is in the news. They also have difficulty putting the information into perspective because of their limited experience with the outside world. If a murderer is on the loose, many five- and six-year-olds will be sure he's coming after them.

It will likely be difficult to shield children from news of national events such as 9/11. But, even information about such widely reported news stories should come through a trusted adult. That adult can help them understand events, using age-appropriate language.

AGES 7-12: PARENTAL GUIDANCE SUGGESTED

If children of this age group are in the room (or car) when the news is on, parents should be especially vigilant for stories that are too graphic for their young ears. They may understand more than we think. Or, they may interpret information erroneously. Be especially careful to shield elementary-age kids from stories of crimes against children. There's no evidence that exposure to these events via the news helps to protect them from harm, and it may make them fearful.

AGES 13 AND UP: TALK ABOUT IT

While young children may think everything will happen to them, teens usually have the opposite attitude. Their belief in their own invincibility can sometimes be tempered by healthy exposure to news about others their age. It's also important for teens to be knowledgeable about current events at a time when you still have the opportunity to give them your take on what's going on in the world. One important exception to this, however, is excessive media reports about teen suicides. Suicide reports have been shown, in some cases, to cause epidemics of suicide. When suicide strikes close to home, it's especially important to talk with teens about what's going on in their lives and how they are feeling. But, talking extensively about the suicides themselves may actually do more harm than good.

When Heroes Fall

OUR CULTURE'S OBSESSION with entertainment and sports personalities ensures that musicians, actors, and athletes are often in
the spotlight. Often, these individuals are very talented in their
chosen careers, but may not be the best examples in other areas
of life. This can be disheartening for kids who look up to their
favorite stars and sports personalities, and may dream of being
like them one day. It can also be embarrassing and uncomfortable for adults when we have to explain indiscretions to children
who thought their heroes had it all on straight.

How do we help kids from becoming disillusioned or cyni-
cal when those they admire are caught in a scandal? And how
can we make sure they are not misled by bad examples? Here
are a few tips for making sure our kids aren't stung too badly by
fallen heroes:

- **Give them heroes they can count on**. Make sure your children know the saints — men and women who lived truly

virtuous lives and can be counted upon to be good examples. Holy cards, medals, and developmentally appropriate books and movies about the lives of the saints can be important tools in encouraging devotion to holy men and women. A good place to begin might be with saints who share the child's name, or saints whose childhood is part of the story. Children are often intrigued by stories of courageous young people who went against the grain. St. Maria Goretti and St. Dominic Savio are excellent examples. Younger children especially often follow our leads. Do we show devotion to saints with whom they might be able to identify?

- **Use a hero's fall to talk about our universal vulnerability to temptation.** All of us have areas of weakness, and all of us sin. Having an unusual amount of talent and notoriety doesn't make people immune to (and may sometimes actually make them more vulnerable to) these human liabilities.

- **Monitor media influences.** Try not to encourage the excessive hype that often surrounds entertainment personalities. Encourage interest in musicians, actors, and sports figures who have a track record of being good examples, especially those who publicly express faith in Christ. While this is no guarantee they will always be a positive example, Christian singers and other personalities are generally less likely to "push the envelope" and publicly engage in behavior that sets a bad example.

- **Encourage your child to seek God's call in his or her life**, and to work to develop his or her own God-given talents. We can remind children that all talents are given to us by God, and that each of us has a special role in God's plan. If kids know this, they are less likely to engage in the type of hero worship that can leave them feeling lost when heroes fall.

- **Reassure your child that he or she can always count on God**. While human beings will continually fail us, God is the same yesterday, today, and forever. He will never let us down.

QUESTIONS FOR REFLECTION ON PART FIVE

What are some fears your child has mentioned or demonstrated? How can you help him or her to have the courage to face those fears?

~

When have you felt you didn't hear the whole truth from your child? What steps can you take to build a relationship of greater openness and trust?

~

How do you handle your child's conflicts with peers? What are helpful and unhelpful ways for parents to be involved in peer conflicts?

~

How much access does your child have to information about current events? How does he or she handle news of tragedies, crimes, or disasters?

~

Who are your child's heroes? How can you encourage healthy role models for your child?

A Parent's Prayer

Dear God, so much is happening in the world around us. It sometimes gives rise to anxiety and fears. Other times, we are tempted to bring into our home conflict from the outside world, or influences from bad examples. Help us to make our home a sanctuary of your peace. Amen.

CLOSING THOUGHTS

Nurturing Marriage
to Be a Better Parent

MANY COUPLES, as they begin to have children, transition away from time as a couple. Their focus shifts to family. The pressing demands of parenthood — the busiest job you'll ever love — push "together time" between husbands and wives to the back burner. Many parents of young children feel guilty about spending time away from the kids — or even wanting to. And the increased mobility of today's families often means that grandparents and other family members are farther away, making it a challenge for many parents to find reliable child care.

Still, research tells us that the best parents are those who take time to nurture the marital relationship, even if it sometimes means occasionally sacrificing time with the kids. This makes sense for three reasons.

First, you are your child's example of how to have a healthy adult relationship. Kids learn by example, so if one of your dreams for your children is that they find good husbands and wived and live "happily ever after," show them how it's done.

Second, children feel more secure when they know their parents' relationship is solid. The day-to-day struggles of marriage and family mean that we will always have some conflicts. Kids get can get confused about how serious these are, and often have fears (even unspoken ones) that Mom and Dad may get divorced because they are arguing. More positive time together for husbands and wives is reassuring to them (and to you) that you still love each other, no matter what.

Third, parents who aren't generally in close communication with one another find it much harder to set consistent limits for their children. Kids often learn to exploit this. They can sometimes pit one parent against the other in an effort to get something they want. (It sounds a little devious, but almost all kids try it at one time or another. Perhaps you remember doing this yourself!) Parents will find that child discipline is a lot easier when they present a "united front." They should work together to give the children what they *need* even when it means denying what they *want*.

So how do we do this in a world of real-life family demands? Here are a few tips:

1. **Ask each other out on dates.** Don't find time, *make* time. Perhaps you could get together with another couple that has young children. You can agree to watch their kids so they can go out if they will do the same for you. Go somewhere you wouldn't go with the kids — a romantic restaurant, a movie. Or, perhaps you may even wish to stay at home and have a quiet dinner and a little romance while the kids are out!

2. **Do the unexpected.** Surprise your spouse with something he or she really likes. It doesn't have to be extravagant. (Flowers are the old cliché, but they still work, guys! They're not that expensive if you deliver them personally.) Perhaps a favorite treat or a love note sent via U.S. Mail to your spouse's work (or hidden in a briefcase or lunch bag). It can take just a few minutes to brighten up a day and spice up your relationship.

3. **Bring back the good old days.** Make a compilation of music the two of you listened to when you were dating. Did you have a song that was "your song"? If you still live in the same city, go to a place you used to frequent together. (If not, perhaps there's a place that reminds you of "home.")

4. **"Steal" some quick moments together.** Make a lunch date while the kids are at school or child care. Be firm about bedtime, and try to spend at least an hour together after the kids go to bed. It should be a time to enjoy one another, not paying bills or folding clothes. Schedule this for two or more nights per week. Steal a moment or two in the morning while you are getting dressed for the day. (Your bathroom door has a lock, right?)

5. **Pray together.** This is another place where time has to be *made,* not found. Hold hands and ask God to bless your marriage and your kids. Pray some traditional prayers together. Take turns reading the Psalms to one another. Tap into the Creator of marriage and family, the Source of the grace that strengthens us as husbands, wives, and parents.

6. **Be affectionate in front of the kids.** Okay, don't overdo it. But giving quick hugs and kisses is nice for you and reassuring to them. Even if they say "yuck," they're probably smiling on the inside.

7. **Be patient with one another.** If you're not already doing these things, it takes a while to "get into the groove." One of you may try something romantic when the other is not necessarily in the mood. Be open and patient as you work to get more in sync. Try again and again.